CW00523655

How No
a Dickhead

*Every Girl's Guide on How Not to
Be Taken for a Ride*

Sarah Levy

First Printing: 2022

Copyright © 2022 by Sarah Levy

All rights reserved.

Printed in the United Kingdom.

This book or any of its parts may not be reproduced or used in any manner whatsoever without the express written permission of the author and publisher. However, brief quotations in a book review or scholarly journal are permitted.

Authors and their publications mentioned in this work and bibliography have their copyright protection. All brand and product names used in this book are trademarks, registered trademarks, or trade names and belong to the respective owners.

The author is unassociated with any product or vendor in this book.

Contents

Free Gift!

Do you know how to easily tell if the man you're dating is a dickhead? Allow me to help you!

As a thank you for reading this book, I'd like to give you a free copy of **'The Dickhead Characteristics Checklist'**.

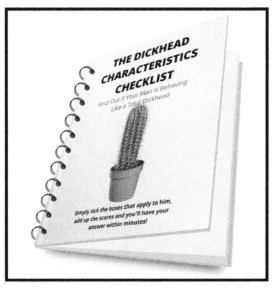

Simply think of how your man behaves, tick the relevant boxes, quickly add up the scores... and in less than three minutes you'll have your answer!

For instant access, go to:

www.the-universal-mind.com/gift

Acknowledgements

Whilst finishing writing 'How Not to Date a Dickhead', I realised that there is so much more to writing a book than just the typing of the words. Without the help of the following people, it could have been a totally different result!

So, my huge thanks and appreciation must go to:

Chris Payne, not only for his endless support, advice, and encouragement during the process of writing and publishing this book but also for telling me in the first place that he thought the subject 'had legs'. Over time, what started out as a frivolous idea of mine – a throwaway, short, humorous book about complete jerks – turned into a more serious, essential guide aimed at helping girls and women wake up to the appalling behaviour some of them put up with from men.

My son, Charlie, and my daughter, Alexandra, without whom I would never have had such a clear insight into the 'next generation' of dating.

My sister, Susan, for patiently reading this book several times during its making. Her suggestions for subtle changes and alternative phrases have turned it into something far better than I could ever have written by myself.

My illustrator, Helal Samrat, for not only his artistic skills but also for his endless patience each time I requested changes to his illustrations.

My cover designer, Ken Leeder, who admirably rose to the challenge of designing a cover that didn't involve coming up with the obvious! Somehow, he managed to produce something that was very apt yet was still within the realms of decency!

My best friend, Sandra, who roared with laughter when I told her the title and subject matter of the book that I was writing. My thanks go to her for saying that she wished I had written the book two decades ago. I do too!

The many dickheads that I've met over the years. Not just in the world of dating but in all aspects of life. It's been helpful to draw on my memories of them as I wrote this book.

And lastly, one particular young man who, out of common courtesy (and a misplaced sense of decency!), I will not name. His dickhead behaviour was the worst I had ever seen.

He was undoubtedly the inspiration for both the title and the subject of this book, and most of the chapters were modelled on him and his selfish ways. I can only hope that he is older and wiser now and has learned from his many mistakes. (Either that or I feel very sorry for any woman that he may be with now!)

About the Author

Sarah Levy is a self-confessed recovering personal development addict. What started as a 'mild interest' turned into a consuming passion, fuelling her thirst for more knowledge.

Becoming a mother to two children gave her an even bigger insight into the workings of the human mind and how limiting beliefs, unknowingly soaked up by a young mind, can go on to be major handicaps later in life – sometimes even decades later.

Her keen observations of life (which she unashamedly calls attending the University of Life) often led to frustrations about people's lack of knowledge about how the human mind works.

Seeing the disastrous dates that some of her friends got caught up with was the only prompt that she needed to write this book.

Whilst it is a deviation from her usual style of writing, she felt that it was a book that just had to be written!

Sarah lives in a small coastal town in England, not far from where she was born and raised.

When not at her desk, writing, she indulges in her passions of music, and escapism through films and stories.

Whilst gazing at the stars on a dark night doesn't help her to write more books, she finds it to be a wonderful way to get life back into perspective and to curb her desire to spread the 'Transformation Comes from Within' message. (It also beats housework and weeding!)

Chapter One

Why You Need This Book

Why You Need This Book

Close your eyes and think about your lovely man. Isn't he simply wonderful?

Think of all the lovely times that you will share in the future, the memories that you'll build…

Dreamy, isn't it?

It's so easy to fall for his charms and to know that you have found 'the one'. He clearly 'loves' you and you love and adore him in return.

Life couldn't get any better, could it?

That's wonderful for you… but what if it got worse?

What if your new love turned out to be a dickhead but you just couldn't see it?

No problem!

You could just turn a blind eye to his faults, knowing that love will conquer all. You just *know* that everything will turn out fine in the end, don't you?

Or maybe you think you'll change him.

It's a classic thing that every girl thinks that she can change a man but they rarely succeed.

And how would you feel if it was the other way round. Would you want him to be trying to change *you*?

Anyway, maybe it will turn out fine in the end... in which case I wish you all the best...

But maybe it won't...

And then what?

Hard as it is to hear it, sometimes you just need somebody to point out the glaringly obvious to you... and that's what I'm here for.

I'm no cacti expert but I know a prick when I see one.

I wrote this book as a guide for all you girls out there who need someone to show you what you are blind to.

To show you all those things that you can't see for yourself.

To help you work out if he's a dickhead or not.

As the saying goes:

'I'm no cacti expert but I know a prick when I see one.'

You will too by the time you've finished reading this book!

Maybe you'll already know a lot of these things (in which case I must ask, 'Why are you still dating a dickhead?') but there will be new stuff as well.

I've included things that are so subtle that you might never notice them or see how wrong they are in your relationship… until somebody points them out to you.

Don't feel bad about it.

You're here for a reason.

Something called you to this book and, now that you're here, let me show you how to turn things around and head off down a different path.

I've Got the T-Shirt

As you might have guessed, I have been there, done that and bought the t-shirt.

Yes, I know what it's like to date a dickhead!

In my younger days, I dated a bloke who I really thought was the right one for me and I somehow managed to be blind to all his faults.

My parents could see them, my sister and my friends could see them… but, of course, I couldn't.

Yes, I had *Dickhead Dating Blindness*!

When I was dating this guy, I thought he was the bee's knees. All the while though, trouble was bubbling away quietly beneath the surface.

I knew things weren't right but I thought he would change.

I didn't want to be single, so I hung on in there, frantically papering over all the cracks, even though they were getting wider by the minute.

Then one day, after a few years of this nonsense, something in me snapped.

I finally realised that this wasn't how I wanted my life to be. I woke up to the fact that I had a choice… Put up with it or get out.

Deep breath… decision made… It was time for him to go!

So, I made the decision there and then. Enough was enough and my boyfriend was suddenly my ex-boyfriend!

Was I upset? Yes, of course, I was… for about an hour or so!

Then suddenly I felt a huge sense of freedom, as if a great weight had been lifted from my shoulders. I was free to do what I wanted, when I wanted, see who I wanted… oh, it was wonderful!

I couldn't believe how stupid and blind I had been … and you'll probably feel the same once you break free of the Dickhead Dating Trap.

To be honest, I can't say that it was any one thing that made me break up with him.

It was an accumulation of things that slowly built up over time until that fateful day when suddenly it was just one 'wrong' thing too many. The criticisms were coming more often, the immaturity was show-ing more and more, and the sulking was just downright childish.

I was starting to feel more like his mother than his girlfriend!

So... deep breath... decision made... It was time for him to go!

Since those young and foolish days, I've seen girlfriends fall head over heels into that trap, dating such unsuitable men that, at times, their naivety left me speechless.

As my son and daughter grew up and started dating, I was very pleased that there were no major disasters there. Nothing that caused me to bite my tongue and keep my opinions to myself!

It didn't stop me from observing people in public though.

So many times, I saw couples who really didn't seem to be 'together' at all. They hardly spoke to each other. They rarely looked at each other.

There was no physical contact between them and not a smile in sight. It made me wonder why on earth they were together. What did they get out of the relationship? It certainly didn't look as if it was happiness!

Then just occasionally I would see a couple who obviously had 'the magic'. They would look so right together, behaving almost as one rather than as two individual people, and their love and respect for each other just shone around them like a halo.

More on that subject later but, for now, let's get back to what you're here for...

To find out how not to date a dickhead.

This Book is for You

So why should you read this book?

Whatever your situation, single or struggling with dating jerks, this book is for you.

If you're dating a dickhead now, then this book will help you to see the reality of the situation you're in.

I'll prompt you to have some respect for yourself and to finally see the guy for what he really is!

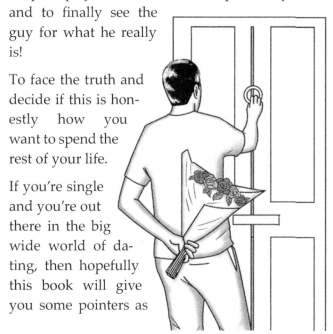

To face the truth and decide if this is honestly how you want to spend the rest of your life.

If you're single and you're out there in the big wide world of dating, then hopefully this book will give you some pointers as

21

to whether your new date is really the man you'd like him to be – or even the man he pretends to be.

Don't get sucked in by his charms and fall into the Dickhead Dating Trap.

You're worth more than that and you know it.

Don't be the person who gets to the end of their life and has merely existed rather than lived.

Instead, be the kind of person that people admire. Shine all your qualities out there into the world so that you can attract like-minded people into your life.

Be the kind of person who knows that they want to improve their life, who reads this book rather than shelves it, and who goes on to act on it, and reap the rewards.

We're going to look at the reality of dating a dick-head and, more importantly, how you can stop doing it!

Laugh with Me, Cry with Me

Breakups are hard… but so is suffering the pain of a relationship that's limping along and isn't going anywhere.

To acknowledge the truth, to admit to yourself that you've perhaps made a mistake… it takes courage. And with that truth, you might find that your feelings start to run deep.

Or maybe the opposite will happen.

Maybe you'll be able to see the funny side of it and laugh at how silly you were to ever get caught up with such a man.

So, laugh with me, cry with me.

Cringe with embarrassment with me if need be. I won't mind.

Let's not get hung up about our feelings and emotions. They are what they are.

Let's just get it all out in the open and be realistic about what you've been up against here.

Start to acknowledge the things about your date that will soon become blatantly obvious to you but that you hadn't wanted to see up until now.

Come on, join me as I point out all those things which you know aren't right about him, but you couldn't bring yourself to admit.

We can be serious together and we can have a laugh together.

Above all else, we can go through the minefield of dating mistakes in a way that will bring you safely out the other side, confident in the knowledge that you are never going to make those stupid mistakes again.

Stick with me and by the end of this book you will know everything there is to know about how not to date a dickhead.

You owe it to yourself, don't you?

Let's weed all those dickheads out of your life and clear some space so you can allow a decent man in at last!

Chapter Two

What Exactly is a Dickhead?

What Exactly is a Dickhead?

The dictionary definitions seem to be quite varied but one thing's for sure... It's not a compliment!

I think we could both agree that 'dickhead' is used as an insulting term of address for people who are stupid, irritating, annoying, contemptible or ridiculous.

It's usually aimed at men (because of the origin of the word, presumably – let's not even go there!) and, these days, it's come to describe a person's behaviour and attitude every bit as much as their personality traits.

Another definition I found is:

> *'A person who is an idiot and shows it all*
> *too well.'*

That sums it up nicely, I reckon, and would have been a perfect description for my boyfriend from my youth!

The Telltale Signs

A first date can often be a bit nerve-wracking for both of you but if you can be on the lookout for the telltale signs on that first date, and act accordingly, you could save yourself a lot of heartache down the line.

A dickhead's dreadful behaviour is usually so obvious that you'd be hard pushed to miss it.

But it's easy to get distracted by the excitement of a new date, a new love in your life… and you may not even see what's going on right in front of you that first time.

However, if you can get past the initial excitement and observe your new man a little closer, these are a few of the things you should be watching out for:

- Rudeness
- Arrogance
- Lack of punctuality
- Lack of consideration
- Selfishness
- Loudness
- Showing off / full of himself
- Talks but never listens
- Lack of respect

Obviously, the list could go on and on, but these few things alone should be red flags for you, especially if several of them are applicable to him.

I'm not saying that you should give him up after the first date if he's not turning out to be quite what you'd hoped for.

After all, people can change their behaviour once their faults are pointed out to them... but it's rare.

By all means let the relationship contin-ue and see how things unfold but, whatever you do, don't be totally blind to how things really are. And don't be afraid to walk away if you realise he's not the man you'd like him to be... and probably never will be.

You may be wondering why some men behave in such a dreadful way.

I can't answer that, I'm afraid, but a lot of it will come down to their upbringing. We learn so much as children, soaking up information, and watching

29

the way our parents behave, in order to learn what type of behaviour is acceptable.

It goes without saying that if a boy sees his parents repeatedly being rude, selfish, or inconsiderate (especially towards women), he is going to grow up thinking that this is normal behaviour.

He will copy that behaviour and think nothing of it. It's only when he starts to mix with others outside his home environment, where people have different expectations, that he'll find that other people find this behaviour totally unacceptable.

Is He a Dickhead? How Will You Know?

This book is about dating mistakes, so let's start with some of the most common traits of a dickhead boyfriend or partner.

Some of them might seem obvious to you but remember that, if you're dating a dickhead, the chances are that you are blind to some of these. You may be caught in the 'Dickhead Dating Trap' and not be able to see the reality of your situation.

It takes courage to answer the questions honestly but please try your best. If you can, be prepared for some harsh truths being revealed to you – ones that you probably chose to ignore up until now.

So, answer these questions truthfully. There are no right or wrong answers, only the reality of your current situation.

It's nothing to be ashamed of either. I just want to shine some light on things for you so that you can begin to see a clearer way ahead. Once those Dickhead Dating Trap blinkers are off, trust me, there'll be no stopping you!

When you're with a man, I'm sure you have certain expectations of how you think he should behave, both with you and towards others. The two of you won't necessarily agree on all of them but most people have basic standards in their minds that they feel others should live up to.

Failure to meet those standards or expectations can only lead to disappointment.

Before you answer the questions below, think about how your boyfriend/partner is with you.

Think about his behaviour, his attitude, and all the things that don't sit quite right with you. Then, take a couple of deep breaths and dive into the questions.

There are no right or wrong answers, only the reality of your current situation.

I've included some real-life examples from women who were all in unsatisfactory relationships, and the things that they put up with before they realised it was time to ditch him.

31

You'll see how bad behaviour can show itself in all aspects of everyday life, from major issues right down to little niggles that you may hardly notice at all but which soon mount up and become too much to bear.

So, let's look at how to find out if your boyfriend is a dickhead or not.

Here we go...

When He's With You

- Does he show respect for you?

- Is he attentive?

- Is he proud of you and does he show it?

- Is he supportive?

> *Cheryl was sick of Craig's attitude towards her. Everything about him was 'Me, me, me,' and he never tired of talking about his latest promotion at work or how his colleagues thought the world of him.*

> *She thought that he might show some pride for her when, on a night out with him and friends, Cheryl announced that she had won the 'Employee of the Month' award at work. But all Craig did was to make a pathetic joke about it and belittle her in front of her friends.*

Communication

- Does he text you daily and does he reply to your texts in good time?

- Does he return your phone calls?

- Does he let you know if he is going to be late?

- Does he involve you in making plans for your time together?

- Does he say he's listening to you but you know he really isn't giving you his full attention?

   Jessica was keen to tell Robert her wonderful news as soon as they met up but it soon became obvious that he wasn't properly listening to her.

   After a series of half-hearted nods from him, followed by a grunt or two, she tested him by saying, 'Oh, and I forgot to tell you that my mother has turned into an alien, and the doctor says that I will need a brain transplant as soon as possible, otherwise I will die within two weeks.'

   When Robert said, 'That's great!' and gave her a false smile, Jessica knew that it was him who was the 'alien'. They spent the rest of the evening in silence and Robert never knew why.

Privacy

- Does he look at your phone without your permission?

- Does he write on your Facebook page without your permission?

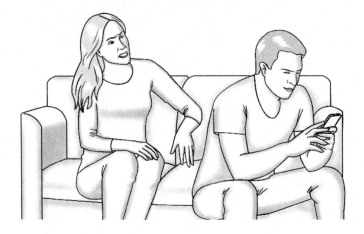

Punctuality

- Is he always late?

- Does he say he's on his way but still takes ages to get to you? (And where did he go or what did he do en route to get delayed, that he didn't tell you about?)

- Does he 'forget' to let you know if he's going to be late?

  Steven's excuse of 'I had to help my nan after she had a fall,' didn't really cut it with Donna, when he failed to turn up to take her to the cinema.

  In this age of technology, surely he could have found time to send a text or make even the briefest of phone calls to let her know what had happened?

  Yes, things happen that throw us off our intended course but, whatever has gone wrong, common courtesy should still rule.

Friends

- Does he dislike your friends?
- Do his friends dislike you? (Could he have told them some untruths about you, to put them off you?)
- Do his friends take priority over yours?
- Does he like you seeing your friends?
- Does he try to stop you from seeing them?
- Does he ignore you when he's with his mates?

*When Katie and Matt were with her friends,
she always made the effort to include him in
the conversation. But she hated going round
to Matt's friends' houses as it was always
the same.*

*They all sat around smoking weed and talking
complete rubbish, while she sat in the
corner, not wanting to join in with what
she thought was a filthy habit.*

*How she longed to have an Invisibility Cloak
so that she could sneak up and bang their
heads together, to try to knock some sense
into them. But what good would that do?
She was already as good as invisible to him.*

Priorities

- Does he call at his mate's first instead of coming to yours?

- Does his addiction to playing video games (or any other 'important' activity) take priority over speaking to you or seeing you?

- Does he think more of his dog/pet (or anyone else) than he thinks of you?

- When you are together, is he always on his phone?

When Daniel constantly 'checked' his phone when they were together, it was the final straw for Lydia.

He would greet her enthusiastically, plant a quick kiss on her cheek and then ask how her day had been. But as soon as she started telling him her news, his hands went back to his phone, his eyes flicking down and back up, as if she wouldn't notice.

There's nothing that shouts, 'I'm not interested in what you're saying,' quite as loudly as a man who is more interested in his phone than he is in his girlfriend!

In General

- Does he overspend on gifts, in an attempt to impress others?
- Does he try to take back gifts he has given you?
- Does he fail to keep promises he's made?
- Is he jealous and insecure?
- Are his excuses pathetic and obvious lies?

  'There was a traffic jam.' 'The dog needed a walk.' 'I couldn't find my car keys.' 'I had

to put some petrol in the car.' 'You never said what time to meet.'…

Rachel had heard every excuse under the sun as to why Andrew never got to hers on time.

But when he was late for Christmas dinner with her family, even though he only lived down the road, it was the final insult.

How she enjoyed watching him suffer as he struggled to eat the main course which must surely have been getting cold and dried up by then, with all eyes upon him as he forced the food down.

How Are You Feeling Now?

I could give you more questions but I think that's enough for you to be going on with. It's quite a list though, isn't it?

It needs to be, for there are many different aspects to a relationship.

I didn't want you to think that everything was fine in one part of it but then find that you hadn't really given any thought at all to a completely different part of it.

So how are you feeling now?

Upset?

Dismayed?

Foolish?

Or maybe you're starting to feel enlightened, empowered and confident.

Whichever it is, it's all good.

(If you want to go the whole hog and you'd like even more questions to answer, you can download '**The Dickhead Characteristics Checklist**' at:

www.the-universal-mind.com/gift

(Don't forget though, you've got to be honest when giving your answers!)

If you answered the questions truthfully, it might have been a bit of an eye-opener for you.

That's alright, it's nothing to worry about.

Hopefully, your eyes have been opened to the reality of your situation and you no longer have the distorted view of the relationship that's probably been your 'truth' up until now.

So, what's next then?

Ditch him?

Stick with him?

Not sure?

That's OK. Take your time.

You need to be 100% sure of your decision rather than rush in at full speed and do something that you regret later.

Chapter Three
What Do You Dream Of... and What's Your Reality?

What Do You Dream Of... and What's Your Reality?

Are you dreaming of true love? Do you have romantic ideas of how things will be once you've found your perfect man?

The thing is, if you've only ever had bad relationships and have never experienced the ease and bliss of a truly loving relationship, how will you recognise it if it comes along?

I'll let you into a secret…

If you think you've found 'the one' you won't need to do any analysing or deep thinking. You won't need to interrogate him or watch his every move to figure it out.

Why?

Because you'll just know if things are right.

As long as you trust your instincts, you'll know – deep inside – that things are right.

However, if you're reading this, it's probably safe to assume that you've never had a truly great relationship with a man. You may have thought and dreamed of it many times but perhaps you've never experienced it.

In which case, if you have no idea of just how good things could be, here's a little taste of what you could look forward to when you meet Mr Right.

What a Healthy, Loving Relationship Consists Of

Love – You love each other unconditionally and you're not afraid to tell each other. In fact, you take great pleasure in doing so.

Honesty – You are completely open and honest with each other. Apart from surprise gifts or parties, there is no need for secrets. Honesty builds trust and strengthens the relationship.

Respect – You have total respect for each other. You treat each other as you would want to be treated yourself. You value each other and you understand each other's boundaries.

Trust – You trust each other fully and give each other the benefit of the doubt.

Support – You willingly and lovingly support each other in all aspects of life, good or bad.

Communication – You can talk to each other freely and honestly, without any embarrassment.

Loyalty – You are totally loyal to each other.

Finances – You discuss finances openly and honestly.

Equality – You are equal partners in the relationship – the perfect team! Any hint of control in any area means that the relationship is unbalanced.

Empathy – You feel each other's pain and do everything that you can to understand the other person's problems.

Tolerance – You are tolerant of the differences between the pair of you. Nobody is perfect and you both recognise that.

Possessions – You have total respect for each other's possessions. No one person's things are 'more important' than the other's.

Privacy – You respect each other's need for privacy when required, without feeling suspicious or jealous.

Individuality– Your identity should not be based on your partner's. You agree that neither of you should have to compromise on who you are, for the sake of the other one. After all, it was your individual uniqueness that attracted you to each other in the first place.

Understanding – You take the time to understand what the other might be feeling. You are open to trying to see things from the other person's point of view to help with this process.

Healthy Sexual Relationship – You are both comfortable with your sexual relationship and you ensure that neither of you ever feels pressured to do anything that you don't feel happy to do.

Space – You recognise the need for a healthy balance between time spent apart and time spent together.

Appreciation – You show regular appreciation for each other, even if it's only in little ways like a 'Thank you,' or leaving a love note on the pillow.

Physical Contact – You both readily give and receive kisses, cuddles, hugs, and other physical contact. Always done appropriately, you sense how something as simple as the gentle touch of a hand on an arm or holding hands can help at difficult, emotional times.

Laughter – You make each other laugh. One of the most undervalued parts of a loving relationship is the ability to make each other laugh.

Please don't be put off by this long list. Maybe you're thinking, 'How on earth can I have all of that in a relationship?' Don't worry.

The chances are that, when you meet the right person, all of this will fall into place automatically. It's all part of the magic of meeting 'the one' and having a loving relationship that seems to work almost by itself, with very little effort needed from either of you.

The Most Primal Urge

I couldn't write a book on dating without mentioning sex!

It's the most primal urge, driving us to procreate and continue the species. Of course, the bonus is that it can also be great fun! The endorphins that are released in your body during sex can become very addictive!

Sex is a wonderful thing! There is something extraordinary about the sex drive. It's like a drug that we want more and more of, and that's fantastic when it's part of a loving relationship. We like being touched, we like the attention and it makes us feel good. It's a reassurance that we are worthy of love.

47

However, if your sex life is with a dickhead of a partner, then think about what's really going on.

Even if you feel that things are great with him in bed, how does that fit with how he treats you outside of the sheets? Because of the addictive nature of sex, are you going back to your far from perfect partner because there is this primal need in you, and you are hooked on the experience?

Perhaps you feel that it is better than nothing... and maybe it is... but what does that say about you?

What do you think about yourself for doing that?

Maybe the honest answer is, 'Not a lot!'

So, perhaps now you can see that sex is only one part of a healthy, loving relationship. To be with someone yet not be able to share the healthy relationship elements that I listed earlier is like living a half-life. You will be missing out on so much and will never be able to experience how fulfilling a loving relationship can be.

What's Your Reality?

Have I left you feeling a little unsettled with all this talk of loving relationships?

Maybe that's a good thing, particularly if you're dating a dickhead and you're not happy with the way things are going.

What is it about him that doesn't feel right with you?

Have you expressed your concerns to your family and friends?

So many times, we insist on charging ahead with an awful relationship and we completely ignore what everyone around us is saying. Perhaps now would be a good time to ask them what they really think of your boyfriend!

Assuming that they've met him (and if they haven't met him, *why* haven't they?), ask your parents and your brothers and sisters what they think of him. Ask all your girlfriends. Ask your work colleagues. Ask everyone if they like him.

In fact, take it one step further and get them to write their opinions down. Sometimes we can easily ignore the spoken word if it's not what we want to hear. So, get them to write it down on paper, or send you a text or an email. Then there will be no denying what they said!

Now...

Let's see what they all say…

Oh, what a surprise! They all say that there is something about him that they don't like. They don't think he's a nice guy and they think that you should dump him. They also think that you are worthy of someone better

Think about it...
Can all your friends be
wrong?

and you don't deserve to have all this unhappiness piled on you.

Maybe your family and friends are all really worried about you. They have concerns about this man and they are worried about your welfare.

Is that a bit of an eye opener for you? I hope so!

So, what happens now?

Are you going to believe them or are you going to dismiss it all as petty whingeing? Even jealousy, perhaps.

The evidence is all there in front of you, so take a good, hard look. All these people – who love you and care about you – are all saying the same thing to you. They don't like him and they think you should dump him!

50

Come on, think about it...

Can all your friends be wrong?

That's so important I'm going to ask you again...

> *Can all your friends be wrong?*

I doubt it, somehow.

Amanda's Story

You're not the only girl in this situation, you know, but sometimes it helps to hear from someone who's been there and come out safely on the other side.

Amanda dated a dickhead for two years before she came to her senses and ended the relationship.

It's no coincidence that she dumped him after finally listening to what her friends and family had been saying all along. She realised that it was indeed highly unlikely that all her friends could be wrong!

Here's what she had to say about life after she ended the relationship:

> *'I finally left him and now I wonder why I didn't do it sooner. But, hey, I'm out of it now.*
>
> *I felt such an idiot because it was only when I left him that I realised what a fool I'd been for staying so long.*

51

After a couple of months, I met somebody who treats me far better. Like a princess, in fact. Now I know what it feels like to be truly loved and cared for by somebody.

And it's really weird because I can't get used to it…

I keep looking at this guy, wondering if he's for real!

Sometimes I say something stupid or, like the other day, I broke a glass and I was waiting for him to shout at me or walk off in a huff.

And it's so weird that he doesn't. He just smiles and gives me a hug. It's so not what I've been used to.

And now I'm wondering why the hell I didn't listen to everyone right at the start! I could've saved myself so much heartache.'

Chapter Four
When Things Go Too Far

When Things Go Too Far

When I first had the idea to write this book, I was going to make it a humorous book, simply listing all the dreadful behaviours that these dickhead boyfriends have.

My aim was to point it out to you, just in case you couldn't see it for yourself, which I know a lot of girls can't.

But as I started writing it, I realised that there was a bit more to it.

Exactly why did girls continue to date these dickheads?

Why couldn't they see what was going on when everybody else could?

My research showed me that often it was more about what was going on in the girl's mind than in the boyfriend's.

A lack of self-worth was usually behind her decision to stay in a relationship that obviously wasn't working and wasn't anything like she had dreamed of having.

Suddenly my humorous book had turned into a more serious one. I wanted to get the word out to these girls and let them know that only by loving themselves could they realise that they deserve better than this dreadful treatment from a man.

Then, as I got further into my research, I realised that there was a very fine line between the dickhead behaviour that I was originally going to write about and abusive behaviour.

So, although this book is still primarily about watching out for those warning signs that tell you that your man is a dickhead, it's only fair that I touch on the more serious side of things as well and mention abuse within a relationship.

The Various Types of Abuse

Sadly, abuse in relationships continues to happen – to both men and women, and nearly always behind closed doors. At first, we tend to think only of physical abuse but there are many different types of abuse.

- Physical abuse
- Sexual abuse

- Psychological abuse

- Financial abuse

- Discriminatory abuse

If you've been fortunate enough in your life to never encounter any of these types of abuse, then you probably won't know much about them.

But you should always know the warning signs so that you can get out of a relationship before any abuse starts to escalate.

Everyone deserves to be treated with kindness and respect, and there is no room for abuse of any kind in a loving relationship. There are no excuses either.

Gaslighting

Gaslighting is a technique that slowly undermines a person's perception of their reality, making the victim eventually question their own judgement, memory, and state of mind.

Quite often the perpetrator will lie habitually and distort the truth. Even when the victim knows that he is lying, they can still end up doubting themselves.

Long term, this can lead to major personality changes and a loss of individuality.

Gaslighting behaviour can include lying, denial, blaming, distraction and minimising. It is a form of manipulation that can lead the victim to suffer from anxiety, depression, and even suicidal thoughts, such is the impact on their mental stability and their sense of self.

Coercive Control

Not all abuse is physical. It can come in several guises.

Coercive control is a form of psychological abuse in a relationship, in which power is exerted over a victim through controlling and manipulative behaviours.

This can leave them feeling controlled, isolated, dependent, or scared.

The emotional scarring is even worse if gaslighting is involved.

It starts slowly, is subtle and increases until the victim can do hardly anything without getting the perpetrator's permission first.

Typical coercive control behaviours are:

- Isolating you from your friends, family, and pets

- Closely monitoring your activity and movements (possibly even using a tracker)

- Controlling your finances and limiting your access to money

- Forcing you to live by their rules

- Threatening to harm you or even kill you

- Policing your lifestyle (e.g., telling you what to wear)

- Gaslighting you

- Denying you your freedom

- Depriving you of access to help (including medical help)

- Repeatedly putting you down and calling you names

- Damaging your property or getting rid of your possessions

Again, this list is not all inclusive.

Please, Please Be Aware!

The various types of abuse make pretty grim reading, I know, but it's only by becoming aware that such things exist that you will be alerted to any signs of abuse in your own relationship.

So many girls walk blindly into a new relationship, 'knowing' that he is 'the one', only to be hit by the harsh reality of life with an abuser, several weeks or months down the road.

And by that point, it's sometimes too late.

It can be too late to get out of the relationship easily, it can be too late to walk away unscathed and sometimes it can be too late to leave the relationship safely, without having to involve the police and the authorities.

So please, please, *please*, if you do just one thing in a new relationship, make it this…

Be totally honest with yourself.

Don't ignore what you're seeing, feeling or how you're being treated. Don't think that you must be imagining it. Don't assume that it will get better and don't feel that you have to put up with it.

If something feels wrong, it probably is.

If he doesn't want to be introduced to your friends, ask yourself why. What is he hiding or trying to achieve? He may very well be trying to isolate you. Please don't ignore that warning sign.

If you no longer feel as confident as you used to, and you start to doubt your abilities, it's most likely being caused by the actions of your partner. Please don't just ignore it.

If you feel that he is trying to control you and take away your independence, it's not a healthy relationship.

> *If it's not a healthy relationship...*
> *You need to get out of it!*

If the relationship is very one-sided and you feel that your thoughts and opinions don't matter anymore, it's not a healthy relationship.

If you find yourself walking on eggshells all the time, making sure that you 'get everything right', it's not a healthy relationship.

If you feel frightened of your partner and are scared that they are going to hurt you or your family, it's not a healthy relationship.

And if it's not a healthy relationship...

You need to get out of it!

End of. No arguing. Call it quits as soon as you can, before things escalate further.

Now I appreciate that it's not always that easy to leave.

You may be living together, and the control may have escalated to a level that has left you totally reliant on him. It's not within the remit of this book to give you advice on what to do in that situation. All I will say though is this...

Ask for Help

Don't be afraid to ask for help. Your friends and family would be the obvious people to reach out to first and they'd probably be only too glad to help you, once they realise what the situation is.

There are also numerous organisations that help victims of abuse.

Plus, there are free phone-lines where you can get confidential advice, day or night.

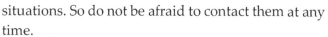

And if you ever feel that you are in danger, you must call the police.

Domestic abuse is being taken much more seriously these days and the police are experienced in handling these sorts of situations. So do not be afraid to contact them at any time.

If you need them, make that call.

Dickhead or Abuser?

I hope that I have not scared you by talking of abuse in relationships. That was never my intention but I would be doing a disservice to you if I had not mentioned it.

Hopefully, you will now realise how important it is to keep your eyes open and be aware of what's happening in any relationship and how it's developing.

Now I'm not saying that all dickheads will eventually become abusers. Neither am I saying that all abusers started off with the slightly less harmful behaviour of dickheads.

What I am saying is that perhaps there is a fine line between the two.

After all, any behaviour that is insulting, offensive, disrespectful, or inconsiderate of another person's rights, feelings and emotions is wrong, whether it is extreme behaviour or more subtle.

So always be alert to anything in your relationship that feels wrong. Even if you can't name it yet. That doesn't matter.

After all, who is the best person to look out for you, if it isn't you?

Always take care and put yourself first.

Now let's get back to why you're here and look more at the problem of dating dickheads, why it keeps happening to you and what you can do about it.

Chapter Five

The Hidden Reason Why You Keep Dating Dickheads

The Hidden Reason Why You Keep Dating Dickheads

I bet you and I have both looked at other couples at one point and wondered what the hell the two people were doing together.

'Why is he with *her*?'

'What on earth is she doing with *him*?'

And so on…

Some couples appear to be really 'together' whilst others look… well… wrong! Just totally wrong.

It's very hard to look without wondering why they are together. We'll never know, of course, but it doesn't stop us thinking.

It may just be that their outward appearance as a couple doesn't tie up with your own values and expectations as to how things 'should' be in a relationship.

Incidentally, you need to be aware that your own values come from various sources, with many coming directly from your own family and friends. We all think that our family's values are 'right' because we absorb them as part of life when we are very young. But keep in mind that there is no 'right' or 'wrong' in life. Things are how they are.

So maybe things are just fine with that couple you're looking at, even if it doesn't look that way to outsiders… and that's OK.

However, …

What if it was *you* that people were looking at? What if you were out with your boyfriend and people were having these thoughts about the two of you? How would you feel if you knew that was going on?

You see, if you're dating a dickhead and you're perfectly happy with doing that (or you've not yet woken up to the facts!), then you'll probably think that you look like a couple that is doing just fine.

But other people will be able to see that something is wrong with your relationship. They will see how you behave with each other; they will notice the body language and it will be obvious to them that all is not well.

If you're perfectly happy with him (for the time being, anyway!), that's fine.

But if – and it's a *big* if – you're *not* happy with him, if things don't feel how you would like them to feel… well, you know what I'm going to say next.

You're not going to 'look' right to others. You will be that couple that people glance at and think 'Why is she with *him*?'

How does that feel now, knowing that people might be thinking that about you?

Not so good? I thought so.

What's Going On?

It's time to dig a little deeper and see what's behind all of this.

I'm going to start by assuming that you're a decent, honest person. You treat other people well and you appreciate how good it feels when others treat you in the same way.

But here you are, plodding along in a relationship with a man who is far from ideal. Some of his behaviours annoy you, you find his attitude far too offhand at times and his manners leave a lot to be desired.

> *Why are you still with him? Could it be because you don't love yourself enough?*

So why are you still with him?

Do you even know?

When I was dating my dickhead boyfriend, things weren't too bad at first. We were getting on OK, and it was nice to have somebody to go out with. But after a while, the annoying things became even more annoying. The know-it-all attitude became wearing. The lack of manners left me feeling angry.

I could go on but I'm sure you know exactly what I'm talking about. You're probably feeling the same way too.

So, I ask again…

Why are you still with him?

I'm going to be brave here and say that I think it's because you don't love yourself enough.

I certainly didn't. I went along with my dickhead's many bad ways because I didn't know any better. Dating was new to me, and I hadn't cottoned on to the fact that I didn't have to put up with all of this.

I didn't have enough respect for myself to realise that I should have been speaking out.

I should have said that there were certain things that I didn't find acceptable. I should have classed myself as an equal.

In other words, even though I didn't realise it at the time, I wasn't treating myself well.

This then begs the question…

If you don't treat yourself well, if you don't think highly enough of yourself, how can you expect anyone else to treat you well?

Now don't get me wrong here. This isn't about you becoming big-headed, feeling more important than anyone else or behaving as if everything should be about you. You don't need to be the centre of attention all the time.

No, what I mean is that we are all equal.

It doesn't matter what we look like, what our background is, how much we earn or how well educated we are…

We are still all equal.

And, in that respect, we all deserve to be treated equally.

If we are behaving decently, then we are worthy of respect and courtesy in return. End of.

So, if you don't feel that you're on an equal footing with the man that you're dating, and you feel that he is treating you as if you were inferior to him, what are you going to do about it?

No need to answer that just yet. There's plenty of time later in this book for some serious soul searching.

In the meantime, though, just have a little think about it.

Because the reason why you continue to date a dickhead – or perhaps you continue to date one after another – could very well be that, deep down, you feel that's all that you deserve.

So often in life we make choices that match how we feel inside.

It may be a subconscious thing that we're not aware of, but we act in a way that matches our internal view of ourselves.

For example, if you feel that you're not very pretty, you might subconsciously choose to date a man who is not particularly handsome.

Why? Because you don't feel that you're worthy of being with a handsome man.

Why? Because you don't feel pretty enough.

The fact that most people are just 'ordinary' in looks yet still manage perfectly well in life (and have some stonkingly good relationships as well!) doesn't even come into your thoughts.

It's as if you're getting by on autopilot, keeping your glass ceiling low because you don't feel worthy of breaking through it.

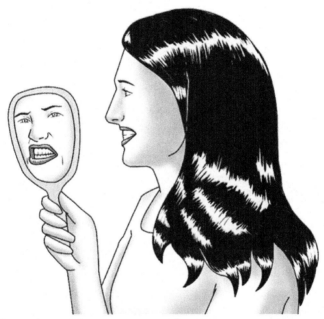

Does that make sense to you?

So perhaps, just perhaps, you might be continuing to date dickheads because you feel that you're not worthy of anything better.

How Do You Feel?

A big giveaway is how you feel about your date.

73

- Do you feel embarrassed to be out with him?

- Are you happier on days that you don't see him?

- Do you look forward to seeing him?

- Do your best friends like him?

I don't really need to analyse your answers to these questions. And you don't need to think much about it either but if you're still not sure, tell me this...

Do you really want a relationship with someone that you're embarrassed to be with?

What does the fact that you are happier on your days away from him tell you about the state of things? Be honest with yourself.

And why would you be going out with somebody who you don't look forward to being with?

Could it be that you are stuck in a rut, afraid to walk away and branch out, in case nobody else wants to date you?

Maybe.

Imagine how your life would be if you were dating a man who respected your feelings, didn't embarrass you and who you couldn't wait to see again.

How would your life feel then?

Aren't you sick and tired of feeling that you're stuck in these rubbish relationships?

Any decision you make in your life is your decision and yours alone, of course.

So, I'm not going to try and tell you what to do or think.

All I want to do is give you a little insight into what might be going on beneath the surface.

You really are worth more than this, you know.

You deserve to be treated with respect and you deserve to be loved by someone who will be on your wavelength and have values the same as yours.

Chapter Six
Your First Step Towards Moving On

Your First Step Towards Moving On

I was going to call this chapter *'Open Your Eyes and See the Bleedin' Obvious'* but then I thought that might seem a bit harsh! After all, if you're under his spell, you're not going to be able to see things exactly as they really are.

I get that completely. I'm on your side, remember? I know only too well what it's like to be caught under that spell!

However, the facts are still the same.

You really do need to open your eyes and see your true situation. Hopefully your answers to the questions earlier have helped you to do that. Without that 'eye opening' exercise, nothing is going to change.

So, I'm guessing that you've now found out that you're dating a dickhead, right?

Is it a bit of a shock or did you inwardly know it all along? (You probably did but you just didn't want to admit that you'd made a mistake.)

Maybe you're wondering what this says about you.

Perhaps you're feeling like a fool, the most stupid person around, embarrassed about how blind you've been to his faults. You might be doubting your abilities and wondering if you'll ever be able to make another sensible decision in your life.

Before you know it, your mind will be rushing away with you, telling you that you're useless as a woman and that no decent man will ever want to love you… You'll never get married, you're going to end up on the shelf, you'll never be able to have a family, you're going to end up as an old spinster...

Stop. Right. There.

That's enough of that sort of thinking! No more beating yourself up!

Put the Bat Down

Deep breath, OK? Calm it down...

Putting yourself down like that isn't going to get you anywhere.

Whatever feelings are coming up for you right now, I want to reassure you that the situation you find yourself in is not your fault.

The most charming of dickheads have a way of making you feel that everything's OK, flattering you when they want to and coming up with 'valid' excuses when they've messed up. It's all part of their nature and the smartest woman in the world isn't going to be able to change them.

At its extreme, when they wheedle you into their lair, this is Coercive Control, which is now recognised in law as a crime. It starts slowly, is subtle and increases until the victim can do hardly anything without getting his permission first. (I discussed this in more detail in Chapter 4.)

> *Pay attention to what your family and friends say about him.*

This is very rare, so I'm not saying this to frighten you in any way. But, please, for your own sake, just be aware of the state of play in your relationship. If you feel deep down that something is wrong, it probably is. Trust your instincts.

Also, please pay attention to what your family and friends say about him. If they don't like him or they criticise him, don't just dismiss it and say they're wrong. Think about it. As I said before, can they *all* be wrong? They may just be seeing things about him that you can't see for yourself.

Anyway, back to you and all those bad things you're thinking about yourself. It's time to stop all that now, you know.

It's time for you to put the bat down. Stop mentally beating yourself up.

Do you hear me?

Stop beating yourself up. Just stop!

You've done nothing wrong. And even if you have (which, trust me, you haven't), it's time to forgive yourself. Stop mentally beating yourself up for your 'wrongs' and put that bat down!

If your closest girlfriend had just realised that the bloke she's been dating for months was a right dickhead, how would you react to her?

Would you tell her you knew it all along?

Would you rub it in about how stupid she's been all this time and tell her what an idiot she's been?

Or would you hug her, tell her you're glad she's seen a different side of him before things got too serious, and tell her that you'll be there for her when she needs you?

The latter, I hope... followed by a big hug!

You need to do the same for yourself. It's about being gentle with yourself, acknowledging the facts and then moving on.

If you wouldn't be nasty and accusing to a friend, then don't do it to yourself.

In fact, the only way that you will make any real headway in life is to be the best friend you could ever wish for.

So, make a start now.

Be Your Own Best Friend

Take a look in the mirror, smile, and say to yourself:

'Thank goodness I've finally seen him for the plonker that he is!

I knew he wasn't right for me, even though I was scared to admit it, but now I know.

It's time to move on with my life and leave him as a distant memory. If another dickhead comes into my life, I'll know the signs and I'll walk away.

83

Big pat on the back to me for coming to my senses… and a hug too, as I'm my own best friend!'

I'll talk later about preparing yourself for a better relationship but, for now, you need to do just these three things…

'Put the bat down', stop mentally beating yourself up, and learn to love yourself again.

The rest will fall into place…

Chapter Seven
How to Break Free from the Dickhead Dating Trap

How to Break Free from the Dickhead Dating Trap

So, is it time to let him go yet? What do you think? Are you feeling more confident about that now?

Are you ready to move on to a more satisfying relationship?

If you've found yourself feeling more and more unhappy about your current relationship, then maybe you have your answer already. No need to overthink things… It's time for him to go.

However, I know that's often easier said than done, and if you look back and realise that you have a track record of dating dickheads, well, it's going to be a lot harder to break the cycle.

You're well and truly caught in the Dickhead Dating Trap.

It is said that it takes 30 to 90 days to break a habit, but this is a habit that will need to be broken in a different way.

Really, it all comes down to one thing...

What you think and feel about yourself.

> *'No, that can't be right,'* I hear you say. *'He's the one who's behaving like a dickhead. It's about him, not me.'*

Well, yes, you're right in a way. He *is* behaving like a total prat... but who has been putting up with that behaviour?

Who has put up with it for goodness knows how long? In fact, how long has it been? Weeks? Months? Years, maybe?

Who has accepted that behaviour by choosing to keep quiet?

Who has gone along with it and not stood up for themselves?

It's you, isn't it?

There is a saying that I love because it's so very true:

'If someone mistreats you once, it is their fault.

If someone mistreats you for a second or third time, it is your fault for not speaking up about it when it first happened.'

Sorry to be a bit blunt with you like that and I really hope that you don't walk away from this book now, just because I've given you the facts. Hang on in there and we can get you through this and on to a better love life, I promise.

It's not a criticism of you and I certainly don't mean it to come across as a blaming game. I'm not saying, 'It's all your fault.' I'm just saying that intolerable behaviour continues because nobody speaks up about it. Fact.

Anyway, enough of the 'blaming'. Let's get on to what you're here for. To find out what you can do about it. I'm here to help, remember?

If you're ready to accept that you had a part to play in this, then let's see where we can go from here...

Honest Answers Only, Please

There are **4 vital questions** that you must ask yourself – and answer truthfully – before you can ever truly break free from the Dickhead Dating Trap.

They are:

1. *What is my honest opinion of myself?*

2. *Do I feel I am worthy of respect?*

3. *Am I less worthy than him (and am I not worthy of something better)?*

4. *Am I less important than him?*

If you want to dig a little deeper, you could also ask yourself:

- *What does my choice of boyfriend say about me?*

- *Do I lack the confidence to stand up for myself?*

- *Why do I put up with such rude and arrogant behaviour from him?*

- *Why do I keep dating dickheads? Is there something missing in my life that I am constantly looking for?*

- *What do I really want in a man?*

It's only when you answer these questions that are all about you and your feelings (and not about him and his behaviour) that you'll be able to finally see what is really going on.

If he's behaving in a way that you don't find acceptable, there are only four options:

1. You speak to him about it, and he changes his behaviour.
2. You speak to him about it, and he doesn't change his behaviour, so you put up with it.
3. You don't say anything, and you put up with it.
4. You don't say anything, and you then choose to end the relationship.

The first outcome would be a great result for you. He sees the error of his ways and is happy to make amends. (Could you get this result for *all* his bad behaviours, though? It's important to take that into account.)

The second and third outcomes are most likely what you're doing now. And, if you're honest with yourself, that's not really how a relationship should be, is it? Is that what you were hoping for and dreaming of when you first met him? Is that what you want for the rest of your life? I doubt it.

Then we come to the fourth outcome, the one that is almost inevitable if Outcome 1 doesn't happen and you're no longer prepared to go along with the other ones.

Which outcome would you prefer right now?

It's Not Such a Secret

Perhaps by now you've realised that there is no big secret to breaking free from the Dickhead Dating Trap.

It all comes down to two things:

1. Realising that you've been choosing to put up with his bad behaviour.
2. Admitting to yourself that you're not prepared to put up with it anymore.

So where do you go from here?

If you've finally accepted the reality of those two facts, there are only two choices. Put up with it or move on.

Your choice.

(Please note that in no way am I telling you what to do. I'm just giving you some guidance as to how to make your own decision.)

Once you see the situation for what it really is, then surely your way forward becomes a bit of a no-brainer, doesn't it?

Chapter Eight
It's Time to Ditch Him

It's Time to Ditch Him

So, have I convinced you yet?

If you truly care about yourself and you now realise that you are every bit as important as he is, then surely it's time for him to go now, isn't it?

Still not sure?

OK, perhaps a little more soul searching is required first…

When I looked back to my dickhead dating days, I realised that there had been warning signs all along. And it wasn't that I hadn't seen them. It was more that I had chosen to ignore them.

So, are there things that you are choosing to ignore?

More than likely.

Big Red Flag Warning Signs

What's that you say? You didn't see any warning signs...

Are you sure?

The 7 red flag warning signs listed here are not at all subtle. They're in your face, shouting at you, glaringly obvious, especially to other people. Maybe you're seeing them all the time in your relationship... or maybe you're choosing not to see them.

Maybe you are so used to people treating you badly that you don't see the signs in the way that other people see.

Either way, seeing them in print can sometimes make all the difference and bring the reality home to you.

So, does any of this sound familiar to you?

1. You feel embarrassed to be seen with him.
2. You're always much happier on the days that you don't see him.
3. You no longer look forward to dates with him.
4. He frequently behaves as if he is superior to you, particularly in public or when amongst others.
5. He seems to delight in putting you down in front of other people, especially when with friends (both yours and his).
6. You find yourself comparing him with other men, even ones that you don't know.
7. You feel as if you are dating a child in a man's body, such is his behaviour.

Do any of these strike a chord with you? Do you recognise aspects of your own life in any of these questions?

Do any of them feel a bit too close for comfort? Or perhaps it felt painful to realise how true to life the questions were.

If so, you know what I'm going to say next, don't you?

It's time for him to go!

It's definitely time to ditch him… and fast!

Now I'm not going to give you advice or ideas as to how you go about that. Only you can decide what's best for you and your situation.

All I will say is that, for your own sake, it's something that you need to do as soon as you can. And be very firm when you ditch him, so there can be no misunderstandings. Don't let him behave as if the breakup hasn't happened. Don't let him talk you round!

This toxic relationship is doing you more and more harm each day that it continues, and I think you know that now.

Chapter Nine

If You Can't Quite Let Him Go Yet

If You Can't Quite Let Him Go Yet

Sometimes in life we know what we must do, to make things right, but we still don't do it. Why? Ah, that's the big question!

There could be all sorts of reasons but one of them is often a lack of confidence. It's one thing to think and talk about making a decision but it's a completely different matter to feel confident enough to act upon it.

Maybe you've now realised what a dickhead your guy is, and you know that he's no good for you.

Perhaps you've realised it's time to move on and that you need to ditch him... but you don't quite have the nerve to do it yet. If that's how you feel right now, that's OK. Don't worry about it (and don't beat yourself up, remember?).

What you need in the meantime is a way to begin to stand up for yourself, that gradually builds your confidence until you feel in a good enough place to make your move.

The FAST Method

My FAST Method takes away that 'doormat' feeling. You know the one? All those times when you feel invisible, as if you're being trodden on and ignored. Those times when you feel like part of the furniture, someone to be treated with contempt.

When you're feeling that the guy has zero respect for you, you'll know it's time for FAST!

No matter how good things may be at times, eventually there will come a time when he does something to annoy you:

- Maybe he'll check your phone when you didn't say he could

- Maybe he'll put a smart-arse comment on your Facebook page

- Maybe he'll be late for a date for the third time running

- Maybe he'll criticise your choice of clothes

- Maybe he'll turn up for a date looking shabby and dirty

Whatever it is, you'll know it when it happens.

It will be the final straw, an insult too far, and something inside you will snap. Perhaps you'd have kept quiet previously but, now that you've read this book, you know better, don't you? You'll more than likely have a hard job keeping quiet!

You know you're worthy of more and you're not going to tolerate his rude behaviour anymore. You may have put your bat down at last but there's nothing wrong with picking it up again as a special treat for him!

So, here it is.

The FAST Method:

F is for Feelings. Acknowledge your feelings about what is wrong. You may be feeling annoyed, embarrassed, or just downright pissed off with him about his behaviour or attitude.

A is for Anger. Be angry about what he's done or said. Think of the injustice of it and don't just gloss over it. For once, really let it get to you. Allow that anger to simmer.

S is for Speak. Speak out about what's made you angry. Tell it to him straight and don't be afraid of any comeback. He'll be shocked at first but that's his problem, not yours.

T is for Think. Sit back and think about how good you feel, now that you've gained your confidence and spoken your mind. (T is also for Trusting the process, as your confidence builds further and further each time.)

Feelings ~ Anger ~ Speak Out ~ Think and Trust

As simple as that (though maybe not quite so simple to do until you get your confidence!).

If you're thinking that you'd like to use the FAST Method, it might be an idea to first rehearse, in your head, what you're going to say to him.

Think about what he might say back to you and have a response already clear in your mind.

Then he won't be able to catch you on the back foot by saying something that you weren't prepared for.

When it comes to the moment, if you need a minute or two upfront to psyche yourself up for it, that's fine.

If you need to take a few deep breaths and count to three before you speak out, that's fine too.

And maybe, if you're really bothered by the thought of speaking out, you should ask yourself this question first:

What's the worst thing that could happen?

The Worst-Case Scenario – Allegedly!

If you speak your mind, what's the worst thing that could happen?

Now let's see…

What might happen?…

- **He walks out on you…** *Oh, good!*

- **He refuses to give you a lift home…** *Always make sure you have enough money on you for a taxi.*

- **He shouts back at you…** *So what? Let him shout. A noise can't hurt you. No need for you to stoop to that level.*

- **He has a tantrum…** *How amusing!*

- **He stops talking to you…** *Enjoy the peace and quiet!*

105

- **He decides to end the relationship...** *Result!*
  (That's saved you the hassle of doing it!)

OK, so my responses to these various 'bad' outcomes might seem a bit flippant to you but you'd probably get the same response from anyone who was looking in from the outside. Others see things that you can't see for yourself, remember?

Many people hang on to a relationship, thinking that things will get better or that changes will happen (as if by magic!) but the reality is usually the opposite.

So, have a little think about it. Open your eyes a bit to see what's really going on and then mentally take a couple of steps back to see the situation how others would see it.

Do you honestly still want to struggle on or does the idea of real love sound much more appealing?

Chapter Ten
Real Love... Are You Ready for It?

Real Love... Are You Ready for It?

So, he's gone at last. The dickhead is out of your life and gradually becoming just a memory. How does that feel? Good?

You bet!

Are you proud of yourself for finally standing your ground and ending it? You've done so well, you know, and I'm proud of you.

So, what's next?

At a guess, I'd say you might be wanting to move on and perhaps soon you'll be thinking about getting back on to the dating scene.

Maybe you just want a bit of fun – a companion to go out with and to socialise with. A person to share your life with but not necessarily one that you want to commit to long-term. That's OK if that's what you want.

But maybe you want more…

109

Maybe you want to meet the love of your life. Perhaps it feels like the right time to meet your dream man, your soul mate, your perfect match....

Whichever words you use to describe him, it doesn't really matter. We both know what you mean.

However, the big question is...

Are You Really Ready?

Are you ready for a deep and fulfilling relationship or are there a few things that you need to do first? A little internal housekeeping perhaps?

You see, it's almost impossible to have a loving and trustworthy relationship with someone if you don't love yourself. Or to put it another way...

How can you expect someone to love you if you don't love yourself?

So many women are caught up in constant self-loathing, focusing on all their bad points and criticising themselves.

They ignore everything that is good about themselves and only see what is wrong. (Well, their version of 'wrong' anyway. In essence, there is nothing wrong with any of us but that's a different story, not within the scope of this book.)

There are so many stories and images of 'perfect' women around these days.

Most of it is fake, of course.

Hyped up stories, 'enhanced' photos, bodies that have seen more surgery than you've had dickhead boyfriends...

It's a hard act to compete with. So don't even try.

It's a fake world, based on lies, and made even worse by social media.

So don't even *try* to match yourself to these images of 'perfection'.

> *How can you expect someone to love you if you don't love yourself?*

Wouldn't you rather be 'you' and live in the 'real' world with 'real' people?

Now tell me one thing...

If you don't love yourself, if you don't feel that you are a nice person with many positive attributes, how on earth do you expect a man to love you?

In your eyes you are flawed yet you want him to see you as near perfect in his eyes – and fall in love with you. (No one is perfect, of course, so don't even think it.)

So how is that going to work out then?

I'll tell you right now. It's not.

111

You can't have things both ways. Either you're lovable or you're not.

I've mentioned this before, way back in Chapter 6, but it's so important that it's worth repeating...

You *have* to put the bat down.

You must stop mentally beating yourself up, going over all your mistakes and putting yourself down.

The negative self-talk *has* to stop, OK?

Learn to accept yourself as you are, warts and all.

Learn to love yourself for the unique human being that you are.

There's no one else like you on the planet so make the most of it.

It's essential that you do this if you are hoping to have any kind of long-term, serious relationship. I can tell you right now, it's very hard to love someone unconditionally when they spend a large part of their day dwelling on their 'faults' and imperfections.

So put the bat down, accept your mistakes, learn to love yourself and move on. There's a whole world out there waiting for you!

Chapter Eleven

Is Your New Love the Real Deal?

Is Your New Love the Real Deal?

So, you've finally ditched the dickhead. Doesn't it feel great?

Time has passed and there's a new man in your life. He's gorgeous and you think the world of him. This time he really is 'the one'…

You hope!

But then maybe the doubts start to set in.

You start to doubt your judgement. You think back to when you first met that dickhead that you were dating, and you realise that things felt good in the early days with him too. And so you begin to think, 'What if?'…

- 'What if he's not the man I think he is?'

- 'What if he's just putting on an act?'

- 'What if he changes?'

- 'What if he turns out to be another dickhead?'

The human mind is great at racing ahead and thinking about the future, throwing all sorts of problems and worries into the mix. (At its extreme, this is called 'catastrophising'.)

The trouble is most of it is made up.

In the same way as the past has gone and cannot be brought back, the future does not exist either. We only have the present moment in which to live our day-to-day reality.

Perhaps, because you are an anxious person, you worry about things going wrong.

Perhaps you were unknowingly 'trained' to be this way because that's how your family think as well.

Either way, it's pointless to keep worrying about the future of your relationship and what might happen.

Instead, focus your attention on the 'now', the time that you spend with him right now.

This is the space and time in which you are going to be able to see if troubles lie ahead or if he really is the real deal.

Remember to keep your eye on the ball though, for any worrying signs or red flag situations.

If you spot any, please don't ignore them, hoping they'll go away.

They won't… and you know they won't.

Make sure that you take off the rose-tinted glasses and see the situation for what it really is. If in doubt, trust your instincts.

Do the sensible thing and call it quits before you're in too deep.

However, if all seems OK so far with the relationship...

Enjoy your time together.

Cherish those special moments that you share, getting to know each other and deepening your relationship.

Build some memories along the way.

Have fun!

Is He What You Want?

Never mind yet about if he's 'the one', think about if he is what you want.

How? It's easy...

When people are asked what they want in their lives, they often don't know. It's as if the offer of an imaginary magic wand makes their minds go blank.

But when you ask them what they *don't* want, they come up with a long list of things!

And this list nearly always includes loads of things that are wrong with their life right now.

They just can't see that, to find what they *do* want in life, they simply have to think of the opposite of what they *don't* want.

So simple really, isn't it?

And you can do the same when it comes to men!

If you used the Dickhead Characteristics Checklist and ticked off all the boxes that applied to your ex, then you'll know what you don't want in a man.

Or maybe you went one step further and made a list of all the personality traits that you'd love your new man to have.

Perhaps you also wrote down how you'd like him to behave and how you'd like to be treated.

However, it's not essential to have done any of these things because you have one very clever thing on your side...

Your instincts.

I think you knew all along that you were dating a dickhead but you were blinded to his faults because you so wanted the relationship to work.

You forgot to trust your instincts and instead you overrode your inner guidance, ignored it, and went your own sweet way.

How well did that work out for you?

Not so good, hey?

Well, now you know better.

That inner guidance is there for a reason – it's there for you to listen to.

So, this time, even though you're probably dying to put ticks on that checklist you made earlier (and who can blame you?), try to trust your instincts instead.

The Simple Way to Find Out

I don't want to make this book more questions than information but, if you're still worried about this, you might care to ask yourself some of the following questions and see what your responses are. Don't overthink it. Just go with the first response that comes to mind. That way it will be an instinctive response rather than a considered one from your logical mind.

Think about times you've spent with your new man and then see what responses come up to these questions:

- How do you feel when you're with him?

- How does he behave towards you?

- Do you feel that he cares for you and about you?

- Is he polite and well-mannered?

- Is there anything about him or his behaviour that unnerves you or makes you feel unsafe?

- Do you look forward to being with him and can't wait to see him again?

Hopefully, your answers will show that your relationship is going along the right lines. If so, keep going!

What is Love?

I thought it would be fun to look up the dictionary definition of the word 'love' but then I discovered that there are so many ways in which the word can be used.

It's not just about love between a couple, as we are talking about here. It can also be love for a child, a parent, a pet, an activity or even an object.

I liked the definition that said:

'A strong feeling of affection and concern toward another person, as that arising from close friendship, sometimes accompanied by sexual attraction.'

Many people find that love develops from what was originally just a friendship.

I also felt that these two definitions matched how most people would imagine a perfect relationship to be:

'To feel or show kindness or concern to a person.'

'To like or desire enthusiastically.'

But this one was the one that really said it all to me:

'People who are in love generally feel a powerful sense of empathy toward their beloved, feeling the other person's pain as their own and being willing to sacrifice anything for the other person.'

To me, that says it all, but I think I would also add the words *'Feeling their loved one's joy and elations as their own'*.

And if you wanted to scrap the checklist completely and not bother with the questions I asked earlier, then take that last definition and apply it to your relationship.

Do you have that empathy for each other or do you not?

Mirror Images

I think I've told you all you need to know really but if you're still dithering, think of it this way...

In any loving relationship, everything should be mutual, and not one way.

Think of the pair of you as mirror images. He respects you; you respect him. He supports you; you support him, and so on.

You are a partnership, not just a couple 'in love'. You are a team and, if you work together as a team, you'll go far. But if you start to pull in different directions, the loving thread will stretch and break. It's inevitable.

Ask any couple who have been married for decades what their secret to a long and happy marriage is, they will tell you that give and take is their main secret to success. That and respect for each other.

But if you need more proof, a recent survey about what makes long term relationships successful came up with 3 things that were the most common:

1. Kindness
2. Generosity
3. The other person makes you laugh.

I couldn't have said it better myself.

You need balance all the way.

If one does all the talking and the other only listens, then it's a one-sided conversation. That's fine in the short term but not in the long run. You may find eventually that one party feels that they can't express any problems about the relationship because the other party 'never listens'.

The lines of communication should always be open and, if you want to make a success of your relationship, you should feel that you can talk to each other about any subject, no matter how difficult or embarrassing.

If mutual respect is there, then you'll know that there won't be any verbal comeback... and that will give you the confidence to speak freely.

Little Things are Really Big Things

I don't want to get into a sexist debate here about how men and women 'should' behave together but if – and *only* if – you like the idea of your man walking on the outside of the pavement when he's with you and he's happy to do it, then go for it, knowing that it will make you both feel good.

Some men like to be true gentlemen with their ladies... and some ladies feel that certain behaviours are a put-down, making them feel inferior. It all depends on what works best for you as a couple.

So don't take these examples as gospel, as everyone is different.

You need to talk openly about any little differences you might have with 'polite' behaviour to ensure neither of you are unintentionally offending the other one. I've just included these few points as things for you to think about.

> *If you're both into holding hands when you're out walking, then do it. It's not an essential but it's kind of nice!*

If he gets to the door first and holds it open for you, and you appreciate that polite gesture, then run with it. And if he's happy for you to do likewise, even better.

Old fashioned good manners, like opening doors, etc., are sometimes down to family training and expectations.

If his family never did such things and yours always did, then you can't expect him to automatically fit in with you and behave this way.

But you could always give him a gentle nudge in the right direction, if it's important to you.

(Look out for his reactions. How he reacts to this may speak volumes!)

If you're both into holding hands when you're out walking, then do it.

It's not an essential but it's kind of nice!

But if you find him striding on ahead without you when you expect him to be by your side, then perhaps a little alarm bell is going to start ringing in your head.

Perhaps you may start to think that he must be very self-obsessed if he thinks that this is an OK thing to do.

These might seem like tiny things but if you have different expectations of what behaviour is considered to be acceptable and what isn't, then it can be the start of a slippery slope if you're not careful.

Sometimes it's the little things that lead to the big problems further down the line.

You have been warned!

If you're still not sure and want to double check, you can download the **'Is He Mr Right?'** checklist at:

www.the-universal-mind.com/gift

So how do you tell if your love is the real deal or not?

Simply look at how your relationship is working.

Does it sit easily with you?

If you feel at ease with each other, have respect for each other, care deeply about each other, can talk openly about anything and always have each other's best interests at heart, I reckon you're on to a winner!

Conclusion

Conclusion

Well, what a journey we've been on together!

We've looked at exactly what I mean by a 'dickhead', the hidden reason why you keep dating them and how to start moving on to someone better.

If you were caught in the Dickhead Dating Trap, I hope that you now feel more confident about breaking free from it.

If you're honest with yourself, you'll know in your heart when it's time to stop putting up with awful behaviour. I hope I've convinced you that you're worth more than that and that you're every bit as good as anyone else.

Letting go can be hard, it's true, but focusing on the possibility of a better relationship should give you the courage to give up on what is wrong and move forward to something better.

I'm sorry if you feel that I've bombarded you with questions. Sometimes, though, that's the only way to get somebody to think properly about their situation and to see it for how it really is.

> *You've put up with dickheads so far... but now you know better. You deserve better.*

Others can say things to you but, at the end of the day, you need to work it out for yourself.

Anyone can read a book like this and pretend to themselves that they've taken it all in and understood it, but it's only by looking inwards and doing the 'internal housekeeping' that you can really start to see what's going on and where any problems might lie.

As a bonus, if you start to improve your relationship with yourself, by acknowledging your faults and increasing your self-esteem, the knock-on effect will be an improvement in many other areas of your life too.

Relationships with friends and family may start to become easier as a side effect of the internal work that you have been doing.

You may also find that work colleagues are easier to get on with and that's always a lovely bonus!

I hope that I have given you a clear enough picture of how real love should be.

There are no hard and fast rules to it, of course. There is no right or wrong about it. Each couple arrives at their own rules.

But I hope you can now see that it is more about how you are with each other rather than anything that society expects of you.

You've put up with dickheads so far... but now you know better.

You deserve better.

You know you deserve better.

You're a great person, so make sure that you see that. Make sure that you get validated by your friends and family. Let them tell you how great you are... and really listen to what they say and believe them!

You deserve to have a great guy in your life… someone who will love you in the way that you deserve to be loved.

Choose carefully.

Choose somebody who will integrate well into your life and who will look after you until the day you die. You deserve it and, deep down, I'm sure you know that you do.

So, go for it, girl!

Go out there and find the love that you so want… and when you've found your wonderful man, drop me a line at **contact.sarah.levy@gmail.com** and tell me all about him.

Tell me how much better things are for you and how you know you've found the real deal.

And, if you like, you can tell me about your dickhead ex as well and how you made the decision to dump him.

I can't wait to hear your good news!

Wishing you a life full of well-deserved love and happiness.

One Final Thing...

If you liked this book, and feel that it has helped you, I would be very grateful if you could spare the time to **leave a review on Amazon, please.**

I'd love to get the word out there to everyone who needs to hear it and I would be very appreciative of any help that you could give with this.

I'd love to hear what you thought about this book.

- Did you like it?

- Was it of any help to you?

- Was there anything you disliked about it?

- Did I miss anything out?

Whatever your views, I'd love to hear from you.

Drop me a line at **contact.sarah.levy@gmail.com** and let me know your thoughts, please.

And, as I said earlier, if you've got a good news love story that you'd like to share with me (or even if you'd like to tell me about your experiences with dating a dickhead!), I'd love to hear from you. If this book has helped you to realise just how lovable and deserving of love you are, then do please tell me.

I look forward to hearing from you.

Printed in Great Britain
by Amazon

34163825R00076